GIVE ME SCOTLAND

By
Jock Tamson

GIVE ME SCOTLAND

Author: Jock Tamson

Copyright © Jock Tamson (2025)

The right of Jock Tamson to be identified as author of this work has been asserted by the author in accordance with section 77 and 78 of the Copyright, Designs and Patents Act 1988.

First Published in 2025

ISBN 978-1-83538-752-8 (Paperback)
      978-1-83538-753-5 (E-Book)

Cover Design and Book Layout by:
    Maple Publishers
    www.maplepublishers.com

Published by:
    Maple Publishers
    Fairbourne Drive, Atterbury,
    Milton Keynes,
    MK10 9RG, UK
    www.maplepublishers.com

The views expressed in this work are solely those of the author and do not reflect the opinions of Publishers, and the Publisher hereby disclaims any responsibility for them. This book should not be used as a substitute for the advice of a competent authority, admitted or authorized to advise on the subjects covered.

A CIP catalogue record for this title is available from the British Library.

All rights reserved. No part of this book may be reproduced or translated by any form or by any means, electronic or mechanical, including photocopying, recording or by any information storage and retrieval system without written permission from the author.

CONTENTS

Introduction 4

Chapter 1 – A Dream Come True 8

Chapter 2 – An Open and Shut Case 12

Chapter 3 – But Why Evil? 17

Chapter 4 – A message in a bottle 24

Chapter 5 – Food for Thought 27

Chapter 6 – Foolish Reasoning 35

Chapter 7 – The True Gospel 39

Chapter 8 – Barabbas Rules – Ok. 50

Chapter 9 – Slay Bells. 59

Chapter 10 – Various Letters 64

    – To the Scottish People 64

    – To the Scottish Government 68

    – To 'King' Charles 75

Scripture quotations are from the New King James Version of the Holy Bible

INTRODUCTION

'Give me Scotland.' - so asked the quiet voice (in my head) as I looked out over the River Clyde from Gourock towards Helensburgh.

It would have been so, so easy to dismiss this preposterous request as coming from my own imagination - as indeed I did initially, but I had had previous validated experiences of God speaking to me through thoughts, dreams and actual circumstances and so, I could never really let go of the absurd possibility that it was God indeed who had asked 'a mere nobody' such as myself to give Him Scotland.

I wrestled with this dilemma for quite some time while simultaneously reflecting on the various ways in which God had communicated with me in the past, and I kept returning to one episode...

It was a sunny, frosty and very still February morning and I had overslept. I awoke and was immediately confronted with the realisation that I had to attend a company meeting in Glasgow later that morning. I rushed to ready myself and, within a short period of time, I was driving out of Gourock.

The journey from Gourock to Greenock was frustratingly slow - but the journey from Greenock to Port Glasgow and beyond was served for the most part by a dual carriageway, and I made far better progress.

On leaving Port Glasgow I quickly positioned myself on the outside lane of the Glasgow bound carriageway and started to accelerate. I don't know what speed I had reached - but it was certainly 'approaching' 70mph.

Within a few minutes the car was very suddenly and very violently buffeted and, in fearful shock, I immediately lifted my foot off the accelerator (on later reflection I found it strange that 'my' first response was not to have instinctively stood on the brake).

As the car gradually slowed, I regained composure and, as I began to absorb my surroundings, the first thing which came to my attention was a massive tangle of skid marks sprawling across both lanes of the Glasgow bound carriageway.

And, no sooner had I observed these than I noticed that three or four cars and a van had earlier left the road, careered down a grassed slope and come to rest against a fence at the bottom of the embankment.

I could not imagine what would have happened if I had hit the black ice moving at the speed I was travelling - but taking everything into account I believe the outcome would have been my severe wounding, or even death.

And, given the fact that my automatic response to the sudden and violent buffeting was not to apply the brake, and considering the stillness of the morning, and the smooth, unbroken surface of the road - my only explanation for the severe, sudden buffeting was indeed 'divine intervention'.

And so, I could never dismiss the 'outrageous notion' that God might have intervened because, for His own reason(s), He wanted me to survive the experience.

But I never directly or knowingly acted on it.

Until the following incident occurred…

It was May 1985, and I was visiting Israel as part of a tourist group led by a pastor who was head of my local church. We had visited many historic sites and, on the occasion to which I'm referring, we had arrived at the Pilgrim Baptismal Site on the River Jordan, whereupon my pastor suggested, because I had recently confirmed my belief in Christ, that I should consider baptism - to which I agreed.

And, in the lead up to my baptism a friend prompted me to relinquish (by way of a token gesture) something which I valued, and since, at that time, I had lost everything which was of meaningful, personal value to me, I decided to give up on my ambition to write - which I did, prayerfully, prior to my baptism.

Not long after my return from Israel - and during a private prayer time, I had an unusual experience - I 'saw' before my closed eyes 'PSALM 45' in bold, white, capital lettering against a dark background.

At this stage in my Christian walk I had little or no familiarity with the Psalms - and in finishing my prayer, I looked it up. To my astonishment the second part of the first verse read: ***My tongue is the pen of a ready (skilful) writer***. Brackets mine.

Could it be that God was giving me back my ambition to write? I asked myself.

And, coming forward to the time of this writing, I decided to read that Psalm again and, for the very first time, another verse imposed itself on my consciousness. It was the second part of verse 4 which stated: ***And Your right hand shall teach You awesome things***.

And, it has since occurred to me that, over the years, I've written many articles - most of which remain unpublished, but all of which (through scriptural study and researching) have taught me so many profound, spiritual truths about the God of the Bible and His relationship with mankind.

Spiritual truths - awesome truths which if accepted and followed by any person, group, society or nation - would beneficially transform that person, group, society or nation. And so, set out in the following chapters, are a few of these 'God given' writings which, if believed by the Scottish people, would indeed give Scotland to God.

And, if ever the nation of Scotland needed to re-accept Jesus Christ back into our society - it is NOW!!

It should be noted that because the following chapters comprise articles written at different times to various recipients - a few recurring themes do occur.

CHAPTER ONE
A Dream Come True

We live in times of great deception in every sphere of human interest - not least in the spiritual domain, as the apostle Paul states:

Now the Spirit expressly says that in latter times some will depart from the faith, giving heed to deceiving spirits and doctrines of demons. 1 Tim 4/1.

God's word is being denigrated as never before and from every conceivable direction.

Before continuing - and because there is a strong element of the 'unbelievable' in this story, it would be good, if not essential, to offer some background information.

Here goes.

A year or so before the start of the events which this story recounts I was led to understand and accept that there is a God and Creator of the universe - and that He is Jesus Christ - and, to those who are brought to believe in Him, He extends a very gracious, loving and eternal interest.

Furthermore, because I believed that Jesus Christ is who He said He is, I had completely renounced and rejected any previous credence which I had in the goodness - or benevolence - or neutrality of all occult practices (mediums, clairvoyants, spiritualists, astrologers, spoon benders, etc., etc.). I had submitted to God's word in ***Leviticus 19/31: Give no regard to mediums and familiar spirits; do not seek after them, to be defiled by them: I am the Lord your God.*** - and held those 'spiritual' practices to be wholly negative, destructive and defiling to the lives of those individuals who were caught in their snare.

A few final points before proceeding with the story:

I'm not a liar - and neither am I given to flights of 'charismatic' fancy - and neither do I hold myself to be anything special - oh yes - and I'm not a self-righteous, holier than thou prig. Those who truly know me will, I hope, confirm these self observations to be true.

And now, to the story:

It was the 6th November 1986 and I had arrived home from work to find my wife, my three children - the family pet and all the furniture had vanished from the house. The only things which remained were furniture marks on the carpets. I cannot describe how I felt - and neither will I attempt to do so - except that to say I was devastated would be the same as calling a Tsunami a small, gentle, lapping wave.

I recall sleeping in a bed that evening - upstairs in the floored attic as I remember.

I don't recall how many nights would have passed after the 'evacuation' - but quite soon, perhaps two or three days afterwards, I experienced a strange dream. In the dream I was walking along a street in my hometown, and as I approached a junction, I was met by my then youngest, eight-year-old daughter, who was walking out from a side street. I was overjoyed to meet her and couldn't get my question out quickly enough:

"Where are you living?"

"You know where I am, Dad," came the confident reply.

"I don't know where you are," I nervously countered.

"Tell me where you're staying - please?" I pleaded more anxiously.

"I'm staying at 7 Davidson Drive," she responded.

The dream finished abruptly. Such was the apparent reality and substance of the dream that I was left with a strong, strong sense that God had spoken to me through it.

In the morning I jumped into the car and headed for 7 Davidson Drive - confident that God, through the dream, had given me my family's new address.

It wasn't - it never could have been - it was a first floor flat in a council scheme - and it was occupied by others.

I am reluctant to dig into the detail of the events which followed - but the bottom line is that the unnatural estrangement and alienation which had been contrived and fostered between my daughters and me continued for many years. From time to time I would get news of their different whereabouts - at one time the younger one was in Southampton while the older was visiting Australia. They appeared to live very nomadic lives - following the whimsical chaos of their own - or someone else's influential initiative.

Towards the end of the 'separation' I enjoyed a secret reconciliation with my older daughter who had returned to live in the area.

One afternoon I received a call from her - she was very anxious and concerned about her health - and her worry seemed to be justified. To cut a long story short - I took her to the local Health Clinic.

I waited in the car - it was a long wait - but eventually she bounced out of the clinic, smiling. On entering the car, she explained the doctor's verdict and cast a prescription note on the dashboard - the patient's name was unsurprising - but the address astounded me. It was **7 Davidson Drive!**

I could hardly believe it. It was difficult to take in - although the natural account of their presence at that address was unremarkable.

Apparently, on returning to the area my daughter had first stayed with my ex-wife at 7 Davidson Drive - which ex-council property her mother had bought on her then recent return from Southampton.

Many years before my estranged family had arrived at 7 Davidson Drive - I was told by God that they would be there.

Why? Why did God give me this information? I believed then it was to strengthen my faith in the hard times which then lay ahead - but now I wonder if it was also to encourage my belief in His then future communications with me.

And it shall come to pass in the last days, says God,
That I will pour out of My Spirit on all flesh;
Your sons and your daughters shall prophesy,
Your young men shall see visions,
Your old men shall dream dreams. Acts 2/17

And there could be yet more to '7 Davidson Drive' than first meets the eye - for this 'terrestrial' location speaks cryptically of another place - a 'spiritual' domain no less.

Although not a scholar in Biblical numerology, I understand that the number 7 is God's number, and therefore, in appropriate contexts, can be related to, or identified with God. The street name is Davidson - the shortened form of 'son of David' - another name for Jesus Christ.

It would appear that God had not only told me where my daughters would be living several years previous to their being there - He had also told me where they might be 'spiritually' - in Him - and that's very reassuring!

Oh yes - another thing - without my younger daughter realising it, she had subsequently moved to live in a house which is situated on the very side street from which she approached me in that dream.

CHAPTER TWO
An Open and Shut Case

How is it possible for any rational person to extend belief in a God who allows such terrible wounding and suffering in the world?

So might ask any intelligent man or woman in the wake of any natural tragedy - or the report of any heinous crime perpetrated by one person or group against another (e.g. the Hamas terrorists' evil and murderous invasion of Israel on 7 October 2023).

And I find myself, at last, confidently rising to the challenge of the question - for, over the years, these armour-clad gauntlets have slapped hard on the ground at the feet of my Christian faith - goading me to respond to their challenge - and taunting me to find the merest hint of weakness in the 'apparent' strength of their case.

Yes - amid all the undiluted evil which has been given life, influence and the cruellest and vilest of ugly expression on this planet - I do sincerely believe that a God of goodness exists and prevails.

And, having just so stated, that saying which speaks of fools rushing in where angels fear to tread - comes anxiously to mind.

Am I being foolhardy in my enthusiasm to take up the gauntlet and attempt to do what some might consider 'the impossible' - to prove God's existence in the face of all the disorder, confusion and outright evil which is prevailing today?

I'll let you judge.

In beginning, can I state, first and foremost, that the irony of all ironies is displayed when an atheist uses the presence of evil to prove the absence of God - because, paradoxically, the presence of evil actually proves the opposite - that God does exist! - And I hope, through this brief discourse, to confront the atheists of academe with the extreme perversity of their logic.

A contrary reasoning which, to reiterate, produces the conclusion that the presence and unrestrained perpetration of evil precludes the existence of a God (of goodness).

As plausible as this assumption might at first appear - and popular as it undoubtedly is (for confirmed atheists are by no means alone in their thinking) it is not based on rational - or logical argument. Indeed, if this line of reasoning was projected into all spheres of life and reality, then the following statements would be true:

A dirty nappy exists - therefore the clean one cannot exist.

An uncontested lie exists - therefore the truth cannot exist.

Cancer exists - therefore healthy tissue cannot exist.

And not one of these assertions is true, indeed, in each case, it is the exact opposite which is true.

The clean nappy exists - therefore the dirty one can and, under 'appropriate' circumstances, will exist.

The truth exists - therefore the lie can and, under compelling circumstances, will exist.

Healthy tissue exists - therefore cancer can and, under conducive conditions, will exist.

It should be noted that in every example offered above it requires the original, pure and perfect 'subject' to be established before its corruption can occur - and furthermore it requires the continued presence of the original subject to uphold and sustain the presence of the corrupted version.

This principle of an established subject co-existing with, and sustaining its corrupted counterpart is witnessed in all areas, and in all spheres of life.

An old wreck of a car can only exist for as long as the reality of the original showroom model remains hidden within, and integral with its battered shell. Remove the reality of the new car from the old car - and the latter can't exist. It is only the car's pristine 'invisible' form which can give reality and meaning to its corrupted 'visible' form. Think about it.

And consider this - a murder can only exist in the context of the life which it has extinguished.

And, in a similar way - a lie or counterfeit can only have credibility for as long as the essence of the original truth, or subject remains hidden within - and integral with its deceiving influence. Separate the 'truth' from the lie - and the lie, in losing its 'credibility and reality' - loses its ability to deceive, and it dies - dead.

As dead, dare I hope, as the atheist's case against the existence of God is fast beginning to appear.

And, there is something else which, I hope, is quickly becoming obvious - that being a universal law which states:

Nothing of a negative value in this temporal/physical sphere can exist without being preceded and upheld by its positive counterpart which, although absolutely real, doesn't necessarily need to be tangible - or visible.

Negativity has no independent value of its own - try looking for the reality of minus six sheep in a pasture unless there were originally six or more sheep in the pasture. Negativity in whatever 'field' it operates can only exist and have a 'real' relevance when coupled with and set against the positive value which it is opposing and attempting to negate or supplant.

To reiterate, it is utterly impossible for a negative, corrupting or evil influence to exist and have a reality without the pre-existence of its original, positive counterpart (which might not be visible) - which is why Jesus Christ could say to the self-righteous and religiously legalistic (sinful) Pharisees of His day – **"The** *kingdom of God does not come with observation; nor will they say, 'See here!' or 'See there!' For indeed, the kingdom of God is within you." – Luke 17/20-21.*

Jesus Christ wasn't complimenting these religious hypocrites on their innate spiritual goodness - anything but - He was confirming the truth that it was a positive and perfect God of goodness working within their sinful, mortal bodies who, for His own (good) purposes, was upholding and sustaining their ungodly and sinful lives.

The apostle Paul must have been aware that the eternal realm upholds the physical realm when, in referring to Jesus Christ, he wrote: **…All things were created through Him and for Him. And He is before all things, and in Him all things consist. -** ***Colossians 1/16-17.***

Yes indeed - our Creator (some naively call Him by the misnomer - 'mother nature') upholds and underpins the entire universe in a life sustaining state of equilibrium - *…and upholding all things by the word of His power…- Hebrews 1/3.*

So there we have it - this negative, evil world with all of its deceit, misery, cruelty, torment, corruption, murder and mayhem can never enjoy an 'independent' reality, or explain itself in the context of itself - because it is negatively orientated and requires a positive value to give it any real presence and meaning.

There are those who will protest that I have unfairly burdened this planet with a negative value - and that it doesn't deserve such offence. To those who might so protest I would challenge them to take everything which this (sometimes) wonderful world amounts to and add it all up - and the bottom line every time will be - decay and death, and you can't get any more negative than that!

As I have stated, life in this world just doesn't make any sense on its own - none - absolutely none.

It needs a pre-existing and co-existing positive value – a perfect, underpinning eternal value **(AND NOT NECESSARILY**

VISIBLE) to give reality, meaning and sense to this negative, temporal and death orientated state: *'for in Him we live and move and have our being,...' Acts 17/28*

To live in this cruel, crazy and evil world - and not believe in a greater being - an absolute life and reality - a divine source of goodness, life and truth is the doctrine of fools, which is why, I suppose, God has said in **Psalm 14/1:**

The fool has said in his heart, "There is no God."

CHAPTER THREE
But Why Evil?

Why did God deliberately expose Adam and Eve (mankind's forebears) to evil knowing that they would succumb to its enticement? Why does all the evil and negativity need to exist - on earth, or indeed - in heaven?

Yes, there is evil in heaven, and No - I'm not courting controversy for the sake of it - **there is** 'evil' in heaven.

God said as much when He admitted to knowing 'good and evil' in ***Genesis 3/22: Then the Lord God said, "Behold, the man has become like one of Us, to know good and evil…"***

If God knew 'good and evil' before the physical creation of the world - as He must have done then, that evil could only have had a spiritual presence and definition - and, as such, could only have been contained within the eternal realm of His Being.

So, how is this possible - and why is it acceptable, on the one hand, for God to accommodate a knowledge of 'good and evil' and, on the other hand, it wasn't alright for Adam and Eve to host a knowledge of 'good and evil'? Because, Adam and Eve - the spiritual forebears of all mankind were banished from Eden for just that - knowing 'good and evil'.

Then the Lord God said, "Behold, the man has become like one of Us, to know good and evil. And now, lest he put out his hand and take also of the tree of life, and eat, and live for ever" - therefore the Lord God sent him out of the garden of Eden, to till the ground from which he was taken. So He drove out the man; and He placed cherubim at the east of the

garden of Eden, and a flaming sword which turned every way, to guard the way to the tree of life." Genesis 3/22-24.

It does seem inconsistent and unjust, but there is a **vital** difference - and it is in discerning this difference that the whole purpose of God - and the reason for His 'apparent' acceptance and indulgence of evil on this planet becomes so very clear.

When it is said of God that He knows 'good and evil' it means that God not only knows 'good and evil' but, more crucially, He knows <u>**the difference**</u> between 'good and evil' - and because He knows the difference between good (those principles which will preserve, promote and enhance His eternal life) and evil (those contrary influences which would erode, negate and obliterate His eternal life) - He can never be deceived by evil into extending them credibility, and therefore detrimental life and influence within His eternal being. Thus evil, while it will remain latent or dormant in the spiritual realm can, and never will have a negating and detrimental influence on His Eternal Life.

On the contrary, with God, dormant evil is continually used for good. As long as 'evil' is recognised by God as 'evil' - its promptings can only ever be used for 'good' - because a knowledge of **evil and the real, tragic and devastating consequences** of following its wicked enticements will always encourage and reinforce God to comply with His own life giving, life preserving and life enhancing principles: An excellent example of this is illustrated in Christ's dialogue with Satan as recorded in ***Matthew 4/9-10:* And he** (Satan/evil) **said to Him, "All these things I will give You if You will fall down and worship me." Then Jesus said to him, *"Away with you, Satan! For it is written, 'You shall worship the Lord your God, and Him only you shall serve'."*** *(brackets mine)*

In other words, God's knowledge of evil is an <u>essential</u> factor in defining, preserving and promoting His eternal life - because, if God holds no fixed and exact definition of who He is (Eternal Life) and therefore has no idea or concept of who He isn't (everlasting death), He couldn't discern between them - and therefore He wouldn't stay eternal very long - would He?

This eternal process of 'knowing evil and the real consequences of following its promptings' can be illustrated at a human level in many ways.

For example, because the fatal effects of fast moving traffic colliding with unprotected pedestrians are universally known, no sane and rational person could be persuaded - or tempted (by evil) to amble across a busy road blindfolded on basis that such an act would add to the length, quality and status of their life. . . .

No, any person so tempted would respond in two ways: firstly, they would immediately reject the wrong thought on the basis that the outcome of following such a thought would be their severe wounding or death - and secondly, they would promptly experience an increase in their resolve to look both ways before carefully crossing the busy road. The net result of which would be 'a life preserved'.

It is the recognition of this process which gives the answer to that age-old question of what the serpent was doing in the Garden of Eden. He was there because God intended to use his negative presence and influence for 'good' - and, I suppose, in that respect - and kept in his proper place, the serpent would always be an agent for 'good' - not evil.

However, Adam and Eve - God's genesis of new eternal life had been beset by a 'different' knowledge of 'good and evil' immediately prior to their expulsion from the heavenly realm.

In the womb - in the Eden of their spiritual beginnings Adam and Eve knew only 'good'. Thereafter, through the 'serpent's' offer of an 'alternative, more attractive proposition', they were introduced to evil. But, they weren't aware that the alternative was evil, and so they believed it - and, in believing it, they unwittingly gave (their) eternal lifeforce to the energising of evil (deceit, disorder and death) within their own eternal constitutions - and, as a result, and as God promised - *. . for in the day that you eat of it you shall surely die – Genesis 2/17,* they (and therefore all the life that God had placed under their dominion) died - end of story. Well not quite, on the contrary - it was the start of 'another genesis' . . .

God never had any intention of giving the serpent (evil) the last word and, as He surveyed the disorder, death and devastation which was once His 'good' creation, and which now lay before Him - *The earth was* (*became*) without form, and void; and darkness was on the face of the deep. And the spirit of God was hovering over the face of the waters – Genesis 1/2,* (*The original Hebrew word 'hayah' can be translated 'was', 'became' or 'had become') He decided to sacrifice part of His eternal life to its restoration and resurrection – *of the Lamb slain before the creation of the world – Revelation 13/8*

Stage by stage, through Christ's eternal self-sacrifice, God would instil His order and life into Adam and Eve's dead dominion - and yes, it would take 'time' - because, as Jesus imparted His eternal power and life into Adam and Eve's dead constitution - He couldn't avoid giving some of that life and power (indirectly) to the evil which was still integral with Adam and Eve's ruined, disordered and dead constitution.

And, in the first phase, as God's pure power (Let there be light) pushed forward to work against the dead resistance of Adam and Eve's now void and formless state - it would initiate the whole process of restoration and resurrection and be met (Big Impact - Big Bang?) by some of His own power as it was being resisted, corrupted and re-directed against Him - via evil's re-energised influences. Indeed, it was this pressure between the positive thrust of God's spiritual power and the negative spiritual reaction which caused the physical precipitation or 'materialisation' of the universe. But that's another story.

And thereafter, in a very real way, God had to travail to progress - He had to continually work against His own corrupted, negative, life denying power (as evil directed it against Him) to create and thereafter maintain the living environment which is this planet in the solar system.

Eventually, in the final stage, mankind arrived on the scene - living human beings who had been resurrected from their dead and void condition, not back to the eternal realm from which they had been banished, but to an intermediate state - a physical sphere of life: ***therefore the Lord God sent him out of the garden of Eden to till the ground from which he was taken. - Genesis 3/23*** - this, our familiar terrestrial plain, the middle ground between eternal life and spiritual annihilation.

Mankind had arrived on earth - mortal men playing host to the divine Spirit of life and truth within, and sustaining them - but blinded to that divine power and presence by the deceiving evil, which was part of their natural, fallen state:

All things were made through Him, and without Him nothing was made that was made. In him was life, and the life was the light of men. And the light shines in the darkness, and the darkness did not comprehend it. - John 1/3-5.

If this is where the story finished - with mankind left to live out his meaningless, mortal life and thereafter drop out of this world into some giant pond of everlasting nothingness - then perhaps the atheist is right and there is no afterlife.

But I, as a Christian, know that there is a God who is moved in everything He does - and everything He permits by His absolute love for, and desire to create new eternal life - new eternal life; who, in having a complete knowledge and experience of evil and its lethal consequences, will know who they are, and why they are - and will never, never in an eternity of years, extend credibility and therefore life, denying influence to the 'evil' option.

At the end of the day - in order to create 'viable' eternal life God has had to allow the introduction and experience of real evil into the developing constitution of that eternal life - He had no choice - absolutely none.

For, how else can 'eternal life in waiting' know evil and experience its hellish consequences - without knowing evil and experiencing its hellish consequences?

And since no 'active' evil is permitted in the eternal realm - the experience of evil had to take place in a separate, derivative sphere - this lower physical state we call planet Earth. . .

But here's the rub, because mankind's thinking processes have been so utterly corrupted by the evil within him, he can have no true and objective means to discern between what is eternally 'good' and what is infernally 'evil'. In effect, no person born of natural, corrupt descent can know what eternal, absolute and unspoilt goodness is - unless God reveals that goodness to him - and thereafter graciously enables him to recognise and accept it.

To reiterate, unless a person can accept and believe in God's definition of 'goodness' - he will <u>never</u> be able to know what evil is.

And to repeat - to the power of ten - the <u>only key</u> to recognising evil is to know what God means by 'goodness'.

Unless we know what true goodness is, evil will always prevail in our self-oriented spirits and lead us down the broad road to destruction: ***Enter by the* narrow *gate; for wide is the gate and broad is the way that leads to destruction, and there are many who go in by it: - Matthew 7/13.***

Christians believe that God has displayed His divine goodness through the ancestry, the birth, the life, the self-sacrifice and the resurrection to eternal life of His Son - Jesus Christ - for all to witness, and for some to accept.

But whoever you believe is the divine embodiment of God's goodness, the truth remains - if you don't know what, or who

God's goodness is - then you won't know who, or what evil is - and if you meet evil and he commends himself to you through the plethora of false gods in this fallen world, as he always seems to do, or he tells you that there is no God, because evil abounds, please remember - he's a liar, upheld by the truth which he's just denied.

CHAPTER FOUR
A message in a bottle . . .

Imagine an artist sitting at an easel painting the landscape in front of her. There, beyond her, is the actual landscape - and close to her, on the canvas, is the artist's painted description - or illustration of that same landscape. We have the physical subject, the actual landscape - and we have its physical representation, the painted picture.

So far - so good.

Imagine Sir Isaac Newton sitting under a tree when an apple falls to the ground at his feet - and the great scientist has that wonderful 'Eureka!' moment when, according to popular myth, he discovers the Law of Gravity.

Sometime later, perhaps after much deliberation, our enthusiastic scientist would have succeeded in writing the description - or definition of the Law of Gravity on paper.

Sir Isaac Newton had the actual subject - the memory of the apple falling under the influence of the Law of Gravity - and he had its physical representation - the written definition of the Law of Gravity on paper. Right?

WRONG, WRONG, WRONG.

He didn't have the actual subject - what he witnessed was an apple falling under the 'influence' of the Law of Gravity. He could not have the actual physical subject - because the Law of Gravity does not have a physical presence. It does not exist physically to be seen - or heard - or touched - or physically represented by anyone/anything.

The Law of Gravity has **absolutely no** physical presence - and yet it has created, sustains and continues to affect and govern the entire physical realm.

Gravity comes upon the physical realm and causes it to react according to its edicts - but Gravity itself is not a physical entity and neither is it contained by any physical entity - you can't bottle Gravity.

It is omnipotent and omnipresent on our planet and in the universe - but it has no physical presence.

And if Gravity does not exist physically - in what realm does it exist?

Could this realm be the spiritual realm - which the atheist scientists are so quick to deny?

I believe that it is.

In the beginning was the Word, (Jesus Christ) and the Word was with God, and the Word was God. He was in the beginning with God. All things were made through Him, and without Him nothing was made that was made. In Him was life and the life was the light of men. And the light shines in the darkness, and the darkness did not comprehend it. John 1 /1-5. *(Brackets mine)*

Comprenez vous?

Do you really understand?

You cannot pour Gravity into a bottle and, what's more - neither can you pour the Gravity out of a bottle. The Law of Gravity - <u>*as with all natural laws*</u>, exists independently from the physical realm - and this can be scientifically proven by using - a glass bottle:

Take any glass bottle with walls strong enough to withstand the effects of atmospheric pressure - and thereafter insert a ball bearing into the empty jar. Please observe that the ball bearing will have fallen - under the force of gravity, to the bottom of the jar. The glass bottle is thereafter sealed by means of an airtight stopper which is also connected via a tube to a vacuum pump. The vacuum pump is then switched on until every vestige of air/atmosphere is evacuated from the bottle.

There now exists in the bottle a small ball bearing surrounded by a vacuum - a space completely void of all physical matter and energy.

Please observe, if the bottle is now turned upside down - the ball bearing will still respond to the Law of Gravity and fall or roll to the top of the jar.

In other words, the Law of Gravity, although it rules the physical realm, exists and operates independently from it.

Comprenez vous?

CHAPTER FIVE
Food for Thought

Once upon a time - a few years ago and from somewhere within the nation's psyche came the voice of one calling in the wilderness. It was the lone voice of the Rev. Jamie Oliver - stirring the peoples' conscience and urging them to repent of the unhealthy food which they had been feeding their children.

And all the people listened - well, a few of them. And there followed great public debate on the nature of junk foods - and the damaging effects which the habitual intake of these foods can have on the health of the human body.

Thereafter much effort was made to devise and promote healthy alternatives. But gradually, amid rebellion in some quarters, all the enthusiasm seemed to fritter out (excuse the pun) and apart from a few sporadic and ever weakening peaks, the drive for healthy eating seemed to flatline.

'Seemed' - but the Rev. Jamie's gospel of wholesome food hadn't been forgotten - his plans to save the health and vitality of our children had been quietly carried forward by those who believed him, and today there lingers an undercurrent of national anxiety - a very sincere concern over the quality of food and amount of sugar which our youngsters consume.

I doubt if there is anyone in the land who won't admire all the effort expended by Jamie Oliver and his like to change the eating habits of our children. Who can dispute, especially in this age of culinary and medical enlightenment, that the continual consumption of junk foods leads to ill health?

Likewise, with excessive smoking, or drinking, or any kind of drug abuse - no person of impartial thought will dispute that the indulgence of any of these practices can be injurious to an individual's physical, or indeed psychological wellbeing.

And, having touched on things 'psychological', it would appear that in this realm too, there is no scientific resistance to the fact that a person's psychological state can be detrimentally affected by exposure to, and intake of a whole host of destructive physical and mental stimuli.

Doctors and psychiatrists straddle the boundaries between physical and mental disorders with effortless ease. They recognise that what affects a person's physical wellbeing can affect that person's mental composure, and vice versa. The term they give to such a process is 'psychosomatic'.

And there, immediately beyond mankind's growing knowledge of psychosomatic illnesses lies a marked border - a very definite boundary, hitherto uncrossed by any serious enquiry from scientists. I refer to that formidable frontier between the 'intellectual' and 'spiritual' realms of human interest.

Mankind the researcher has never scientifically ventured into the religious spheres of human concern. And that is a tragic loss.

For if a person does comprise body, mind and **spirit** - rather than just body and mind, and the health and condition of the body and mind is directly related to the state of the spirit - and vice versa, then it would be better if mankind was able to discern **scientifically** between what is good spiritual food and what is junk spiritual food.

It would be terrible, would it not, to rigorously test the quality of the physical and psychological food which we feed our children, and ignore the quality of the spiritual food which we feed these same children?

Today, generally in western society, our children are taught the salient characteristics of the main religions of the world on the basis that one is as good - or as bad as the other, which means, at the end of the day, a child's choice will boil down to personal preference - based on the whims and influences of ancestral, parental, cultural and media conditioning.

Can you imagine the state of a child's mind if it was taught any subject based on personal preference and prejudice? Yes, we can well imagine the outcome - ignorance and error.

Can you imagine the state of a child's body if it was taught to feed itself based on personal preference?

Yes again, we can well imagine the outcome - rotten teeth, ill health and obesity.

Can you imagine the state of a child's spirit if it has been taught to feed itself on the basis of religious conditioning? No. We can't, we don't have a clue. We have no 'scientific' proof that one religion is better than the other - so we have no basis to make a value judgement between one religion and the other - so we can't possibly discern between good and bad 'spiritual' food.

Wrong!

The scientific man has the ability - **right now** - to make an impartial judgement on spiritual matters - if only he would set aside his natural prejudices, cross 'the great divide' between the secular and the religious and apply his **objective** intellect to it.

The scientist is far more acquainted with the truth of the spiritual realm than his fettered reason has thus far revealed to him - and sadly, the vast majority of 'religious' people are far, far farther away from the truth of spiritual matters than their culturally conditioned beliefs could ever grasp.

If a scientist was invited to arbitrate among all the religions of the world - he would, sooner or later, conclude that, despite some similarities, they were all quite different and, in some instances, very contradictory in their beliefs e.g., Christians believe in Jesus Christ's divinity, crucifixion and resurrection while Moslems only consider Him to be a human prophet and that His resurrection was untrue.

The scientist would have no choice but to reject all of them as possible myth and continue his study from a purely impartial and truthful basis i.e., from scientific fact. But where could he find the hitherto illusive, direct connection between the physical and spiritual realms which would allow him, <u>factually and scientifically</u>, to translate his knowledge - and therefore his informed judgement from one sphere to the other? And, as he pondered this problem, turning it over and over in his mind, day after day, week after week, month after month - he 'might' eventually experience the exhilarating intrusion of a 'Eureka' moment.

Yes, perhaps he might suddenly realise, like a fish which had spent its life swimming the vast oceans of the world looking for 'oxygen', that that which he had been seeking had been an intrinsic part of the body of water which he had been swimming in throughout all of his (re)searching.

Yes, it might be then that he would recognise that the key to the truth of the spiritual realm was the realisation that the myriad 'natural' laws through whose obedient and co-ordinated processing the entire physical universe has been created and thereafter sustained - whilst they have come upon and imparted a constant, order giving and creative power on the physical realm - they themselves, in **pre-existing the creation of the physical universe**, cannot be physical in their essential being. Rather they must belong to, and emanate from a preceding, causative state of reality - dare he conclude - a 'parental', life creating - 'spiritual realm' - a 'Father God' no less?

How could it be otherwise? - Our scientist would admonish himself and further reflect: Take any law - the Law of Gravity for instance, where can the physical 'substance' of this Law be heard, seen, touched, smelt or tasted? This Law's omnipotent, omnipresent and constant power over the physical realm can certainly be witnessed and experienced - and its definition can be written down and accurately reproduced just as a photograph can represent a landscape. But an original landscape exists to be seen and touched - where does the Law of Gravity, whose power is responsible for the existence, development and preservation of that landscape, reside, to be seen and touched?

It cannot be seen and touched because it does not have a physical form. The Law of Gravity (as with all natural laws) although integral with the physical realm, exists independently from it, and so must emanate from a different sphere - a realm 'beyond natural dimension' - a transcendent, primary and ruling sphere - a 'spiritual' realm, as he had previously concluded.

Yes, he might confidently acknowledge - it is the omnipotent and omnipresent 'Laws of Creation' which are, and constitute in their creative, ordered outworking - a true and direct connection between their primary spiritual origins and the derivative, physical universe which they have created.

Without doubt he had found a direct link between the spiritual realm and the physical state, and which link, he contemplated, must be the same as that which exists between the invisible, pre-patterned light beams emanating from a film projector and the two-dimensional, secondary images which they cause to 'materialise' on the opposing surface of an otherwise void and blank cinema screen.

In other words, our temporal, physical environment is a secondary, three-dimensional state 'of reality' which 'materialised' when invisible, authoritative, spiritual laws, in being projected outwards in all radial directions, impacted with (Big Bang?) and thereby imparted their spiritual order, life, energy and identity on, and into the passive and arresting resistance of a hitherto formless, lightless, lifeless medium...

> *The earth was without form, and void; and darkness was on the face of the deep. And the Spirit of God was hovering over the face of the waters. – Genesis 1/2.*

And there began a deluge of consecutive thoughts…

A formless, lightless and lifeless state - addressed and imparted order, energy and life by the authoritative prescription - the intelligent, parental demand - the '*Let there be*' of a whole host of co-ordinated, powerful, life giving laws and processes which had been directed, in creative sequence, by a spiritual intelligence, to impose their identity on it **(Genesis 1/3-31)**.

A spiritual identity which could never be 'singular' in its reality for, as all spiritual laws confirm - the secret of all life and viability is found only within, and radiating from principled, ordered relationships between complementary partners acting in unison: *Let Us make man in Our image* - **Genesis 1/26**.

'Complementary partners' which will **always** meet the following descriptions:

The first partner: the head: The Law - the identifying and authoritative **Prescription** - the genetic definition (of a prescribed product) - the seed, which prescribes the Process to be enacted to achieve the creation of that prescribed Product.

The second partner: the active Aide - the **Process** - the developing seed which opens itself and gives itself to obediently enact the genetic Prescription in order to achieve the creation of the prescribed Product.

The third partner - the prescribed **Product** which has been brought into actual being by the Process giving itself to obediently enact the directions of the genetic Prescription.

The **Prescription**, the **Process** and the **Product.**

One in three - and three in one.

A triune relationship of spiritual origin which constitutes and upholds the essence of **everything** which has been created in the physical realm - across **all** spectrums of life and reality:

…He is not far from each one of us; for in Him we live and move and have our being, Acts 17/27-28.

First the inert, **prescriptive** Neutron - assisted by its working partner - the active, open Proton which gives itself to obediently **process** and thereby project the powerful progeny of its union with the Neutron into a myriad mist of otherwise negative, dead and disordered Electrons - through which impartation process it forms the **product** - **the atom** - the unit base of all physical form.

First the **prescriptive** DNA - assisted by its working partner – the active RNA which gives itself to obediently **process** the powerful outcome of their union into otherwise dead, inorganic matter - resulting in the **product** - **Protein** (the essential base of all cells and therefore all life).

First a cake's (**prescriptive**) recipe - whose instructions are obediently and actively **processed** by the baker - resulting in the creation of the **product** - **the actual cake**.

First the Architect's (**prescriptive**) plans - whose specifications are obediently and actively **processed** by the various tradesmen - resulting in the **product** - **a New Building**.

First the **Highway Code** - whose instructions are obediently and actively **processed** by the road users - resulting in the **product** - **Road Safety.**

First the film's **prescription** - the written script which is obediently and **actively processed** by the actors and film crew - resulting in the **product** - **the actual film.**

First any viable concept - followed by the sacrifice of energy to obediently process that concept - resulting in the birth/creation of the actual reality.

Actual reality - given and sustained by a life-giving trinity - a creative, ordered relationship between equals which must, without doubt, emanate from a spiritual intelligence which must, in turn, constitute the essence of the life of a greater spiritual being - our Creator God comprising Father, Son and Holy Spirit.

In the laws of creation, he had found a direct link between God and His physical Creation. He had found a validating watermark, a constantly repeating tripartite pattern, an infinitely recurring fractal configuration which is inlaid through, and intrinsic to all created life and reality, and patently absent from all 'manufactured' deity.

In other words, that person called Jesus Christ (the second member of the eternal trinity) who, two thousand years ago at a place called Calvary, sacrificed His natural life to obediently enact (process) His Father's eternal Will (the authoritative **Prescription** of Eternal Life) and thereby, through that sacrificial '**process**', retrieved Eternal/spiritual Life (**the product**) for Himself and for those who would believe in Him, can only be, who He said.... He is:

"**I am the way** [the process], **the truth** [the prescription] **and the life** [the product]. **No one comes to the Father** [Eternal Life] **except through me.**" John 14/6. (brackets mine)

CHAPTER SIX
Foolish Reasoning

. . . because what may be known of God is manifest in them, for God has shown it to them. For since the creation of the world His invisible attributes are clearly seen, being understood by the things that are made, even His eternal power and Godhead (divine nature), so that they are without excuse. (Brackets mine)

Romans 1/18 – 20.

Man, the secular, unbelieving scientist - the 'unknowing' recipient of God's life and truth - always striving to discover, harness and employ God's divine principles to improve his lot in this life - but, nevertheless, forever blinded to their eternal origins by his idolisation of, and therefore wrong relationship with the fatally flawed and isolated intellect - an incomplete and lesser intellect which, in operating independently from the greater intellect from which it has been separated, will always have its perception distorted by deception - and perverted by prejudice.

If only the 'atheist' scientist would cease from the sheer folly of denying the reality of God by using the very witness for His presence - as the actual evidence **against** His existence.

This perverted reasoning - this irrational logic - as practised by many of those scientists and evolutionists who continue to stubbornly and strenuously deny God's existence, is sheer lunacy.

That they have rejected all of the religious and spiritual error of this world is highly commendable - but that they should throw the baby out with the bath water - this is not clever - this is foolishness.

Does the spoor of an animal not bear conclusive witness to its presence, or does the hunter track in vain?

Do the fossilised bones of dinosaurs not bear conclusive witness to their past existence, size and form, or are palaeontologists complete fools?

Does a person's very unique fingerprint discovered at the scene of a crime not prove that person's previous and indisputable presence at the scene of a crime, or are forensic scientists idiots?

The thrust of the above questioning is obvious - substantial and irrefutable evidence of any phenomenon's previous or present existence - proclaims and proves that phenomenon's past or present existence, it does not hail and confirm its absence - unless, that is, you are the renowned zoologist and acclaimed author Richard Dawkins, who also happens to be a prominent atheist and eminent evolutionist.

Richard Dawkins has a 'good' mind - but it is human, and it is flawed - as is his logic. During his presentation of the Royal Institute's 1991 Christmas lecture Richard stated that he did not believe that evolution operated in accordance with a Creator's preconceived outcome, but rather the process of adaptation and development (evolution) was the result of a spontaneous response, by the genes which control any animal's anatomy and physiology, to a change of circumstance in that animal's environment. In other words, the process of evolution as it applies to any individual life form does not operate in compliance with a Creator's Prescribed Plan, rather it just makes it up as it moves along.

In an attempt to prove his point, the eminent scientist asked the audience to consider the Flounder. He explained that the Flounder is a 'flatfish' which swims on its side and inhabits the sand and mud of the seabed around the coast of Britain. He further described the fish as having both of its eyes set on one side of its face - and that the asymmetrical - lopsided location of the second eye, together with underlying symmetrical skull formation suggested that expedient improvisation - and not a deliberate design prescription had produced the final form of the Flounder's head.

Richard Dawkins argued that, taking into account the overall anatomy of the fish, it was obvious that the latter had been, at some point in time, an ordinary fish swimming in a normal way - and that this fish, in developing a 'preference' to swim and lie with one side of its body facing, if not touching the sea bed, had to gradually move the position of the eye which was in contact with the sea bed to the upper side of its face in order to avoid irritation and redundancy.

He then concluded that if an intelligent Creator had designed the Flounder - he would not have done so by employing such a clumsy and inefficient improvisation - rather he would have designed the Flounder in such a way that the finished creature would be perfectly suited to and live in full harmony with its environment. Mr Dawkins finally offered the Stingray, or Skate as examples of fish which, in their design and symmetry, were exactly as fish should look and operate - if there was a divine intelligence behind their creation???

Would it have been - and does it remain possible for Richard Dawkins, and those with a similar selective and prejudiced perspective, to see the humble Flounder exactly as it is meant to be seen by impartial and unprejudiced research, and that is, as an **exception**, given by a very gracious God - **which proves the rule**. Such rule being that there is a supreme intelligence behind the creation of the universe - otherwise ostriches, such as Richard Dawkins, might evolve to have eyes on their posteriors.

'God given exception' apart, there is another way to see the humble flatfish and that is as one of those 'delusions' which God promised to visit on those who discount or reject His word: ***And for this cause God shall send them strong delusion, that they should believe the lie: - 2 Thessalonians 2/11.***

Richard's book is entitled *The God Delusion* - and oh, what a divine irony shines through the choice of that title!

And the light shines in the darkness. . . - John1/5

One final thought on the **absolute _absurdity_** *of 'Evolution'-*

Isn't it so, so very strange that **every** created thing (**product**) in this physical world, which the **process** of 'evolution' is alleged to have developed and created, emanates from a parental **prescription** - except for **'evolution'** itself?

Very strange - dare I say – **ILLOGICAL and STUPID!**

CHAPTER SEVEN
The True Gospel

But sanctify the Lord God in your hearts, and always be ready to give a defence to everyone who asks you a reason for the hope that is in you, with meekness and fear; - 1Peter 3/15.

And so, in a world which is increasingly hostile towards Christianity, I now, in obedience to God's call, offer good reason to anyone who would ask me to explain the basis for the very real hope which resides within me.

But first, a little preamble.

Hope?

What is 'Hope', but a confident expectancy of a future improvement in one's present situation.

And what is humanity's present situation?

Well, mankind has always been accommodated in a world which is, in a very real sense, a battlefield between life and death. Truly, everyone who is born into this world will eventually die out of this world - with death, despite tremendous medical advances, always having the indisputable 'last' word.

And, as we all face the inevitable prospect of death's 'apparent' victory, it can be reasonably claimed that the only real, <u>ultimate</u> 'hope' which any person can hold is that they will experience 'spiritual life after their physical death' i.e., a resurrection to eternal life.

But, on whose provision - and on which religious or secular beliefs should any person rest their hope (or otherwise) in such a resurrection?

The choice is immense, truly immense, but despite the many 'religions' of the world, there are only four 'generic' groups into which each can be placed, and these are as follows:

1 Atheists - those who reject the existence of a Creator God and instead worship/focus on the 'god' of their own, or someone else's deceived, self-focused understanding.

2 Theists - those who accept the existence of a Creator God, but reject Jesus Christ as being that God, and instead worship a god - or Allah - or Vishnu - or Buddha - or whoever - or whatever - conceived and born from their own, or some other mortal's very deceived, self-obsessed imagination.

3 *Cultural Christians - those who accept the existence of a Creator and believe Him to be Jesus Christ - but relate to, and worship Him based on their own, or someone else's 'self-preserving and self-promoting' understanding of God and His Word. This category can include Roman Catholics, as well as most Protestant religions such as Presbyterians, Anglicans, Baptists, Pentecostals, Methodists, Charismatics, Episcopalians, Mormons, Jehovah's Witnesses etc.

4 True Christians - those who accept the existence of a God and Creator and have been spiritually enabled to recognise Him as Jesus Christ - and who, thereafter, share a relationship with Him based solely, from start to eternity, on **His sovereign initiative**.

Four categories - but with only **one** of two spiritual powers governing each - there are no hybrids.

And these spiritual powers exist in **direct opposition** to each other. If one power can be defined as life preserving and life promoting - the other (opposing) power, despite a multitude of deceiving impressions to the contrary, can only be described as life denying and death producing.

The first - the primary, positive power has, as its foundation, a true, life preserving and life promoting prescription, or formula, while the other, the derivative, negative power has as its base, a deceiving, life denying and death inducing recipe.

Every person born (**with one unique exception**) has been born enslaved to the secondary, negative power. There should be no argument here, because (**with one unique exception**) every person born into this world will, sooner or later die, be dead - out of this world.

The Bible refers to the first, primary power as 'Righteousness' - which is the God obedient, selfless Spirit (the essence of all reality, truth and life), and it refers to the secondary power as Sin - which is a self-idolising, self-preserving, self-promoting spirit (the base constituent of all delusion, deception and death) - from which, for all humanity, there is no escape…

Yes - no escape, absolutely none - because our natural minds and bodies are Sin bound. We are **all** self-preserving, self-promoting, self-sustaining, self-fulfilling, self-idolising, self-ambitious, self-motivated people who live and die in bondage to our 'sovereign' self-bound wills - and therefore can only exist 'for a time' - in **fatal, sinful (lawless)** rebellion against the righteous, selfless Spirit of our Sovereign God and creator.

The relationship which Righteousness has to Sin can be accurately compared to the relationship which a healthy cell has to a cancerous cell. It's that simple. Healthy cells comprise (life giving) proteins which are produced when a correct DNA prescription is obediently processed by its working partner - the RNA, while cancerous cells are the deadly outcome/product of the RNA processing a wrong DNA prescription …

In other words - as far as our eternal God is concerned, and in the context of eternal life - **every** person born is, essentially, a cancerous cell - and not welcome in His eternal body: *..**and he who does not believe the Son shall not see life, but the wrath of God abides on him. - John 3/36***

A question: If someone invited you to consume a bowl of 'apparently' wholesome porridge, and you knew that it had been prepared with water contaminated with invisible, cancerous cells - would you accept the invitation?

Of course, you wouldn't - and sadly, for all mortal, Sin enslaved, human beings who aspire to go heavenward upon their death, our God and Creator reacts to them as you would react to the contaminated porridge i.e., with total and absolute rejection.

In other words, no matter how 'apparently' wholesome, Godward and selfless your thoughts, beliefs and actions might appear to be (to yourself and others) if they're controlled, contaminated, enslaved and motivated by a self-extolling, self-preserving, self-promoting, sinful, negative power - then God will not admit you into His eternal kingdom, rather He will completely and eternally condemn and reject you.

Not everyone who says to Me, 'Lord, Lord,' shall enter the kingdom of heaven, but he who does the (selfless) will of My Father in heaven. – Matthew 7/21 *(brackets mine)*

And this divine rejection is the destiny for all humanity…

Unless, as some 'self' inspired and 'self'-made *cultural Christians (**wrongly**) suggest…

There exists a way, by and through which a person can, at some point in their life, become **'self'** aware of their total enslavement to Sin and, in **selfish** fear of their afterlife destiny and/or in **selfish** anticipation of their afterlife reward, decide to reject their Sin master (as if they could) and thereafter choose to accept the eternal God as their Sovereign…

At a superficial level, it does seem to be an effective solution - but for one salutary fact. The controlling and motivating spirit lying behind the 'decision' to transfer from Sin to Righteousness is lawless i.e., self-willed, self-ward, self-preserving and/or self-promoting - and so, the 'apparent' transition/transformation from selfish motivation (SIN) to selfless Godward submission (Righteousness) can only ever be, at best, elaborate 'self-deception':

"The heart is deceitful above all things, And desperately wicked; Who can know it? - Jeremiah 17/9.

And so, mankind, motivated by his own sinful (lawless) self-preserving and self-promoting 'free' will is, upon death, irredeemably and incurably dammed to eternal annihilation.

Yes, eternal annihilation i.e., a second death - and **not** the eternal torture and torment of burning in hell forever - as most of **cultural** Christianity has always **wrongly** believed and promoted.

A second **death** is every person's destiny. *For the wages of sin is death, Romans 6/23*

Unless, as God's word confirms…

A mediator exists - one who was and remains the '**unique exception**' referred to earlier. A man who, unlike any other, was born **sinless** and who has never been overcome or ruled by the 'self' focused spirit of Sin. A man who was, and remains submitted to, and therefore empowered by the selfless Law of Eternal life. A man who holds divine authority and power and who can pierce the impenetrable barrier of Sin which incarcerates a person's original, genetic, eternal identity.

A man who has indeed taken the selfless initiative and cut through that otherwise impenetrable veil of Sin between God and Man.

A man who was, and is **the only** mediator between God and Man.

A perfectly righteous man whose name is Jesus Christ. Jesus Christ - who was called by His Father's Will to set His people free (from Sin) and did so through His absolute self-sacrifice and subsequent crucifixion, at Calvary - 2000 years ago:

And He (Jesus) said, "Abba, Father, all things are possible with You. Take this cup (His pending torment, torture and crucifixion) *away from Me, nevertheless, not what I will, but what you will. - Mark 14/36*. (brackets & underlining mine)

Christ crucified at Calvary - which had been planned by God before time began because it is **the only** means through which a person's original selfless and Godward spirit can be reconciled to, and made eternally alive, secure and complete in Him.

Then, behold, the veil of the temple was torn in two from top to bottom; and the earth quaked, and the rocks were split, and the graves were opened; and many of the saints who had fallen asleep were raised; - Matthew 27/51-52

How?

Well, to understand the how, we must first understand the 'why?'

And the 'why?' is best understood at a natural level - before transposing it to a spiritual level:

For since the creation of the world His invisible attributes are clearly seen, being understood by the things that are made, even His eternal power and Godhead, so that they are without excuse. - Romans 1/20

We all know, or should know that, at a natural level, apart from hermaphrodite exceptions, singularity does not and cannot create or sustain life. Where life exists, it exists as the result of the consummation of a relationship between two complementary genders (male and female) who could never be complete in themselves and who are moved to seek that completeness in union with each other.

And, as it happens in the natural state, so thereafter, it occurs in the spiritual realm: *However, the spiritual is not first, but the natural, and afterward the spiritual. - 1 Cor 15/46*

Just as there is only one way for a person to be alive in, and aware of the physical sphere - which is by being conceived (<u>by the</u>

will and actions of another) and born into it, there is only one way for a person to be alive in, and aware of the eternal realm - which is by being spiritually conceived (<u>by the will and actions of another</u>) and born into it.

Jesus answered and said to him, "Most assuredly, I say to you, unless one is born again, he cannot see the kingdom of God." John 3/3.

… who were born, not of blood, <u>nor of the will of the flesh, nor of the will of man</u>, but of God. - John1/13. *(underlining mine)*

We are conceived physically when our father's sperm and mother's ovum are mutually consumed in, and by each other. To put it another way - both the sperm and the ovum must lose their previous individual identities before they can contribute to and become the complete genetic essence of a greater life and identity - with a far greater life span.

Unless a sperm takes the initiative and penetrates the (dead) membrane which incarcerates the ovum its life span is a mere 4 to 5 days, while an ovum will only last 20 to 24 hours on its own - and yet, in being united with, and made complete in each other, both their lives are immediately extended by anything up to, and beyond 85 years.

So, you might ask, how else does natural conception reflect spiritual conception?

As natural conception is the uniting of two separate, but complementary genetic components - so spiritual conception is the coming together of two previously separated, and therefore complementary genetic components.

Two **previously separated**, and therefore complementary genetic components???

Yes, let me elucidate.

'Eternal Life' is, by **definition**, a life **without beginning and without end**. Yes, **without beginning** - let that sink in! And so, **of necessity**, any person who experiences true spiritual/eternal birth while here on earth, **must have pre-existed** their life here on earth in some eternal, conceptual form (seed or ovum).

... just as He chose us in Him before the foundation of the world, that we should be holy and without blame before Him in love, having predestined us to adoption as sons by Jesus Christ to Himself, according to the good pleasure of His will. - Ephesians 1/4.

And that seed/ovum, in being 'eternal', would have had to have been perfect in its genetic constitution - because only a perfect, incorruptible eternal seed would be able to produce a perfect, incorruptible eternal life:

... having been born again, not of corruptible seed but incorruptible, through the word of God which lives and abides forever, - 1 Peter 1/23.

And what, you might ask, constitutes perfect, incorruptible eternal life?

The answer, simply, is one which can sustain and preserve its life - **eternally**!

And what ensures that an eternal life will maintain its life forever?

The answer again, quite simply, is a life which knows the difference between: a) the Godward, **selfless** precepts upon which its eternal life is founded and b) the sinful, self-willed, life denying principles which, if believed, will cause that life to degenerate - eventually to die.

And so, any eternal conception must include within its genetic prescription, planned provision for the developing subject, not only to be taught and experience correct eternal precepts and their outcome - but also to be taught and experience contrary, sinful, deceiving principles and the lethal consequences of their evil outworking.

In other words, a viable eternal conception must, of necessity, include exposure to, and the eventual recognition of selfish evil in all of its tragic and deceptive outworking - otherwise the resultant 'eternal' life wouldn't have the unconquerable compulsion to repel it - and therefore wouldn't stay 'eternal' very long.

To put it another way, the enslavement to evil - and a subsequent deliverance, salvation or redemption from it - is an <u>essential</u> constituent of eternal life.

Therefore, for any developing eternal life to advance to maturity it must first be exposed to and suffer the terrible consequences of being personally and intimately corrupted and enslaved by Sin - and the first and worst of these consequences is **immediate separation** from its eternal Parent.

Every developing eternal life must, for a time, **suffer separation** and alienation from its eternal Parent - but at some later point in its eternal development that life must be **saved and redeemed** from its sin-bound state and, in having its eyes opened to the true nature of the Sin which has enslaved it, be **reconciled** to its original Parent.

But this reconciliation cannot possibly be achieved by a 'selfish' life which is languishing in **inescapable** bondage to Sin (with all its self-deceptions and self-distractions). This reconciliation can only be initiated by the eternal Father who has prescribed the whole creative process and knows that He, and only He has the selfless initiative and power to cut His children free from the deadly membrane of Sin which has temporarily incarcerated them.

Enter Jesus Christ - God in human form who, in obedience to His (Father's) divine will, took the **selfless** initiative and, in dying, to His own natural 'self-will' at Calvary, defeated the powers of selfish Sin and, in so doing, pierced and cut through the otherwise impenetrable curtain of Sin between Himself and His eternal progeny, and thereby became reconciled and re-united, via His Holy Spirit, with the **selfless** essence (ovum) of His children's original eternal identity.

The glorious outcome being the reunion of pure **selfless** partners which secured His children's resurrection to a full and perfect eternal life.

... and the sheep hear His voice; and He calls His own sheep by name and leads them out. And when He brings out his own sheep, He goes before them; and the sheep follow him, for they know His voice. - John 10/3-4.

If you have heard His voice, then Christ's Spirit has already penetrated the dense membrane of Sin which once separated your eternal essence/ovum from His, and in so doing has consummated an eternal relationship with your spirit - and you now share in my hope - the real and certain hope of a resurrection to eternal life - given to us through Christ's Godward self-sacrifice and crucifixion at Calvary.

And if you have heard His voice, all you need do now is repent - turn way from all of your previous religious and/or secular indoctrination/understanding and accept, in and through **His** faith, that you are now, through Christ's self-sacrifice and subsequent crucifixion, reconciled to your God and Creator in Heaven - and thank Him for His self-sacrifice.

I have been crucified with Christ; it is no longer I who live; yet not I, but Christ lives in me; and the life which I now live in the flesh I live *by faith in the Son of God, who loved me and gave Himself for me. Galatians 2/20.

The original King James Bible interprets the phrase 'by faith in the Son of God' - as 'by the **faith of the Son of God' - Big difference!*

Which is the accurate translation?

It was Christ's incorrupt and selfless faith (in God's will) which took Him to the cross at Calvary - believing that He would be resurrected to eternal life after three days and three nights: ***For as Jonah was three days and three nights in the belly of the great fish, so will the Son of Man be three days and three nights in the heart of the earth. - Matthew 12/40.***

In other words, we are saved by 'the faith of Christ' which faith enabled Him to obediently submit His (human) will to his Father's eternal will:

Father, if it is your will, take this cup: *(His pending crucifixion)* ***nevertheless not My will, but Yours be done. - Luke 22/42.*** *(brackets mine)*

CHAPTER EIGHT
Barabbas Rules – Ok.

Not many people are aware of it but, according to some historical accounts, there were two people with the first name of 'Jesus' involved in the unfolding events of Christ's trial, conviction and crucifixion.

There was, of course, Jesus Christ - whose first name 'Jesus' is Hebrew for 'Saviour', and whose second name 'Christ' is Hebrew for 'the anointed one' - and who was named and appointed by God through the angel Gabriel.

And then there was another man whose first name, according to some, and implied by others, was said to be Jesus which, as stated before, means 'saviour' - but whose second name, as agreed by all scriptural accounts, was Barabbas, which means 'son of Abba' - Abba in Hebrew meaning 'father'.

So, there we have them, two men called Jesus.

Two sons - one born from the heavenly realm by the righteous will of God, and the other born from the natural sphere by the mortal, sinful will of man.

Two men - the first a saviour, and therefore propagator of God's eternal life and ancestry - both in Himself and, through Himself, in others to come, and the second, an outlaw, and therefore propagator of his human father's sinful, unrighteous life and ancestry - both in himself and reflected through himself, in others to come.

Two men - who were destined to be presented as a 'choice' to the Jewish people.

At the time of Christ's arrest, the Jewish people were preparing to celebrate their annual religious feast of 'Passover' and, in recognition of this celebration, the Roman governor decided to release to the Jewish people a prisoner of their preference.

And so, the governor of the time - Pontius Pilate, in an attempt to save Jesus Christ who he knew to be innocent of the charges levelled at Him, included Christ in the choice which he intended to offer the Jewish people.

He asked them to decide between freedom for Jesus Christ, the innocent, falsely accused man who stood before him - or Barabbas, already justly incarcerated for insurrection and murder.

To Pilate's astonishment the people were persuaded by their chief priests to have Barabbas released to them.

Why?

Why didn't they prefer to have Jesus, a known man of miracles, life and peace, returned to them?

At a purely human level it is madness - that a people should deliberately and wilfully decide to release murder and rebellion back into their community at the expense of life and peace is irrational. It makes no sense - absolutely none, unless serious cognisance is paid to the instigating and underlying spiritual influences which were controlling, and therefore manifesting themselves through the attitudes, behaviour and words of the main protagonists.

So, who were the main protagonists in this tragic event?

We have the Jewish people:

A people who, according to their own Old Testament scriptures, were seldom at one with their God's precepts of life and freedom - and consequently nearly always in bondage to some foreign power or other - and, at that time, while subjugated to Roman rule, still awaiting the coming of the promised 'Messiah'. The Messiah - a man anointed by God who, again according to their own scriptures, would save and deliver them, once and for all, from the oppression of foreign powers - and, through that deliverance, lead them to realise the fullness of God's promised blessing on their nation.

We have the Jewish priests and elders:

Religious and learned men who (despite being very familiar with the various scriptural descriptions of the promised 'Messiah') had developed their own distorted impressions of how the sum of these scriptures was describing the qualities and strengths of this promised Messiah.

They had desired and were therefore looking for a predominantly 'warrior' King - a mighty champion - one full of human resource and ingenuity who would lead their nation to challenge and engage their Roman oppressors on the battlefield of human might and endeavour.

These priests and elders never grasped for a moment that their bondage to other nations was merely a symptom of an underlying spiritual bondage to the alien gods of these other nations. Seldom, if ever, had they lingered on the idea that their nation's continuing subjugation to foreign powers was a direct outworking of their innate and very human disregard/distortion of God's eternal precepts and principles.

The Jewish priests were unaware that there was no middle ground in the spiritual realm, and that to be separated from God by disregard of His person and precepts was to be united with, and languish in bondage to any - or all of the tyrannical powers of negative spirituality.

And, as a result of this spiritual deception and oppression from which they undoubtedly suffered - and which fed their predominately proud, self-righteous and unrepentant attitude towards God and their own shortcomings - these Jewish priests would never be able to accept, far less retain, a scripturally balanced or accurate impression of their promised Messiah.

These 'men of God' with their deceived and distorted impressions of God and themselves would never seek, nor indeed identify with a 'meek', mainly spiritual Messiah who had, and who ministered absolute power and authority at a distinctly spiritual level - never mind one who would consistently penetrate their proud, self-righteous and religious facades to reveal their truly corrupt spiritual state:

"Woe to you, scribes and Pharisees, hypocrites! For you are like whitewashed tombs which indeed appear beautiful outwardly, but inside are full of dead men's bones and all uncleanness…" - Matthew 23/27.

These Jewish priests and elders did not - and could not understand that their nation had been raised and separated by God as a means through which He could communicate Himself - His eternal truth, presence and spirit to the rest of mankind - the fallen, mortal world of mankind, of which they, although separated from it, remained a spiritually intrinsic and <u>representative</u> part.

They did not understand that they had been chosen by God - not because they were spiritually 'at one' with God, or closer to God than the rest of the world - but because, in their response to Him, they were spiritually typical of the rest of the world.

They did not understand that what made them 'good and superior' was not any intrinsic spiritual goodness which their nation held - but the divine values which God had chosen to express and illustrate through 'their' Scriptures.

These 'learned' Jews did not grasp that they, and their people were as words and pictures on a page - and that they, together with their scriptures and experiences, conveyed and illustrated eternal truths (prescriptions/laws) - without they themselves having the independent ability to be, or to manifest, or to understand - or indeed to obediently process the greater eternal truths/prescriptions which they were being used to illustrate and convey.

They were as actors playing parts of which they had no knowledge and speaking lines in a language of which they had no understanding - because they did not have the means - that 'crucial' spiritual cipher - that eternal associate with which they could engage and who would allow them to translate, process and develop the genes - the language, the symbolism and the intrinsic promise of their religion, and therefore their very own lives, into a properly fulfilled eternal reality.

They were unaware that they and their religion were singularly incomplete and specifically 'genetically prescriptive' in nature. They didn't realise that, while they were intended to be an intrinsic and essential part of a new and greater eternal reality, the confirmation and subsequent development of this 'new life' could only be realised if they and their 'prescriptive' religion (DNA) were introduced to, and united with a complementary (RNA) partner of the same genetic derivation.

They were indeed spiritually blind, and the concept of having to be spiritually re-generated through reconciliation with another of the same genetic derivation to ensure the eternal propagation (salvation) and subsequent development of their spiritual potential would make no sense to them:

Jesus answered and said to him, "Most assuredly, I say to you, unless one is born again, he cannot see the kingdom of God". Nicodemus (a Jewish Priest) ***said to Him, "How can a man be born when he is old? Can he enter a second time into his mother's womb and be born?" Jesus answered, "Most assuredly, I say to you, unless one is born of water and the Spirit, he cannot enter the kingdom of God. – John 3/3-5.*** *(brackets mine)*

Truly, the Jewish priests were blind to their life's purpose and deaf to the message which God conveyed and illustrated through their life's experiences.

And, in not being reconciled to the eternal associate who would allow them to translate their message (and therefore themselves) into the eternal reality of which they and their religion spoke - and since that eternal partner would, at least in part, be very alien, unfamiliar and repulsive to their own self focused and diametrically opposed spiritual condition - then, if and when that eternal associate was presented to them, it would not be unreasonable to expect them to instinctively reject Him, and thereafter retain that with which their fallen natures were most comfortable and most familiar - which is exactly what did happen when they called for the release of Barabbas and the crucifixion of Christ.

After the Jews, their priests and elders - and their hopes of a sword brandishing Messiah, **we have Barabbas:**

[Jesus] Barabbas - a knife wielding rebel - a murdering insurrectionist - some suggest a religious fanatic - a man who had attempted to come against the might of Rome (negative spirituality) with his own might and guile - and failed.

And a man who was far more suited the Jewish peoples' idea of a Messiah than the innocent man who stood before them claiming to be the Messiah.

[Jesus] Barabbas - a saviour - a natural man born from his own peoples' familiar, but wrong ideas of what qualities a Messiah should have.

[Jesus] Barabbas - a man of fallen, negative, spirituality. A son of this world, and of his people - a 'saviour' born to perpetuate his father's ancestry and life at a human level - but still one whose spirit was diametrically opposed to the God whom he claimed to worship and represent.

Finally, we have **Jesus Christ.**

Jesus Christ - the saviour anointed by God - the Messiah whose coming was promised on many occasions and in many ways by the Jews' own scriptures - as illustrated in **Isaiah 53/3**:

He is despised and rejected by men,

A Man of sorrows and acquainted with grief.
And we hid, as it were, our face from Him;
He was despised, and we did not esteem Him.

Jesus Christ - a man not recognised by His own people:

He was in the world, and the world was made through Him, and the world did not know Him. He came to His own and His own did not receive Him. – John 1/10-11.

In effect, what was being played out through the people and events of Jesus Christ's trial was truly a spiritual conflict between two diametrically opposed spiritual systems - a head to head confrontation between the forces of good and the forces of evil - a mighty battle between eternal life and everlasting death.

A contest between two adversaries who would measure their performance - and the resultant outcome by using two completely different value systems.

God - the God of life, light and truth would look on His Son's mutilated, crucified body - and the absolute obedience and self-sacrifice which took His Son to that state and see only His victory - and Christ's resurrection to eternal life through that dead body.

Satan - the god of darkness, death and deceit would look on Christ's mutilated, crucified body - and the lawlessness, deception and injustice which took Him to that state and see only his sordid triumph - and Christ's abject failure in that dead body.

Two systems, defining and claiming their own success at Calvary and, in the process, offering a choice to mankind:

There is eternal life in, through and beyond Christ's physical death or,

There isn't eternal life in, through and beyond Christ's physical death.

There is - or there isn't.

Two systems each declaring their own absolutes: if Christ is alive, He must be alive absolutely, and if He is dead - He must be dead absolutely.

But which system prevailed in the crucified Christ at Calvary?

Transport yourself back to that day on which Jesus Christ was publicly tried. Put yourself in the Jewish crowd, for whether you like it or not - and whether you can accept it or not, every person born is a Jew in the heart of their sinful, unregenerate, human spirit. And, as you stand beside your Jewish brothers and sisters, ask yourself - who would you choose to release into the community?

The truth is - you don't need to transport yourself back to any point in time, because the battle which was portrayed through Christ's trial and crucifixion is constantly playing out. It is spiritually defined. It is timeless and it transcends national identity and religious loyalty. It is a spiritual reality and it exists, in your heart - here and now.

Your choice isn't historical and hypothetical - it is here, and it is now. It is present and it is palpable. It is real, and it confronts the 'Jew' in you at this very moment.

It doesn't matter whether you're a Jewish Jew, a Jewish Protestant, a Jewish Roman Catholic, a Jewish Moslem, a Jewish Hindu, a Jewish Buddhist, a Jewish Pagan, a Jewish Satanist, a Jewish Spiritualist, a Jewish New-ager, a Jewish atheist, a Jewish wokist etc., etc., - whatever type of Jew you are:

Who will you set free in your heart and in your community - Christ or Barabbas?

Two thousand years ago the Jewish Jews chose Barabbas and, about 70 years thereafter, their nation was subjected to a complete dispossession of, and dispersion from their homeland (the Diaspora).

And, 80 or so years ago - the Jewish Jews were subjected to the most evil 'Barabbas' of modern times, aka Adolph Hitler who succeeded, through the holocaust, to exterminate six million Jews.

It would appear that if God was speaking, and is continuing to speak through the Jewish nation (Israel is presently possessed and oppressed by Islamic powers antagonistic to their very survival e.g. Hamas' murderous invasion October 7 2023) then His message is very strong, very serious and very clear:

To reject Christ's peace and authority from any community is to release Barabbas - anarchy and lawlessness into that community.

'Great' Britain, in the name of religious equality, is by quickening degrees rejecting Christ and embracing Barabbas.

This country's once free spirit has become oppressed and possessed by a contending spirit - a threatening, bullying, exacting, murderous and vengeful spirit.

Is this an unfair and unjust appraisal? I think not !!

Consider this country's government - its continual attempts to restrict free speech, its spin, its dishonesty, its promotion of false religion and all its mendacious and corrupt ways - and tell me 'Barabbas' doesn't stalk its corridors of power.

Consider all the lawlessness, the injustices, the murders, the violence, the rapes, the wokeness and all the corruption of education - and tell me Barabbas doesn't stalk our schools and streets.

Yes indeed, Barabbas does walk freely in streets of this country - with increasing impunity.

Through its rejection of Christ - this nation has released Barabbas into its midst. I have no doubt - absolutely none.

BARABBAS RULES - OK, because the Scottish people, in rejecting Christ, have blindly decided and elected to set him free - OK.

Barabbas - the rebellious, lawless, despotic, religious – sometimes 'respectable', sometimes 'honourable', sometimes 'reverend' - always self-righteous spirit of godless man - rules Scotland. And I truly despair.

CHAPTER NINE
Slay Bells.

During the approach to Christmas Day 1995, while quickly flicking through the pages of an abandoned tabloid - which I had stumbled across in some now long forgotten place, I had a strange experience - one which I'd never encountered before, or met since.

Who knows what processes the human mind uses as it attempts to assimilate data which the eyes have gleaned from an over hasty scan of any information presented to them? All I know is that on the occasion to which I refer, my brain must have been working about two or three pages behind its intake of visual information, because my quick browse through the paper was brought to an abrupt halt when the headline from a previously viewed page registered late in my consciousness.

The particular caption which stopped me dead in my tracks was:

SATAN RULES - OK

'Surely not', I reprimanded myself as I quickly backtracked to re-read the heading. And the self-censorship was justified, for the actual wording read:

SANTA RULES - OK

Faced with the evidence of the first word on its second and more deliberate reading, I had no alternative but to dismiss my first interpretation as some form of dyslexic aberration borne from an over-stretched mind. But on hindsight, and as I began to reflect on how the true Spirit of Christ has always been eclipsed to varying degrees by that wretched, unwholesome and self-orientated spirit of Christmas, I started to wonder whether or not my mind had misinterpreted the caption's message.

There, but for the camouflage of one misplaced letter:

Could **SATAN** be the spiritual reality behind **SANTA** - that mythical character with the red suit and white beard who lives at the North Pole?

Could Santa, that 'larger than life' benefactor who 'contributes' to the erroneous celebration of Christ's birth around the time of the winter solstice each year, really be satanic in his inspiration?

Is Santa, Satan's son - a diabolical lie born into this world, via the fecund womb of mankind's naturally godless imagination, to provide yet another diversion from God's true expression - Jesus Christ?

Could it be said that SANTA is the friendly guise and that SATAN is the underlying spiritual malignancy - the instigating spirit behind his progeny's omnipotent, jovial, generous, and totally Christ detracting performances in the two to three months leading up to mid-winter each year?

Is Santa pro-Christ, or is he anti-Christ?

Has the myth of Santa Claus been sired in the minds of men in union with the Spirit of Truth - the Spirit of Christ, or has it been spawned by the imaginations of men in collusion with the father of lies - the spirit of Satan?

God is Spirit, and those who worship Him must worship in spirit and truth. - John 4/24. Would the Spirit of Truth give His seed to the conception and birth of a mythical character who, when fully developed by acquisitive, selfish humanity, would then stand against absolutely everything that Jesus Christ lived and died for?

Is God almighty a fool?

Would God sire and give birth to the only human expression of His Eternal Truth - to His only begotten Son here on Earth, only to encourage the divine light from that truth to be eclipsed in the hearts and minds of adults and children by a lie - by an absurd caricature which has no mortal reality, far less any eternal integrity?

No, God is not a fool, and neither does He give Himself to the fathering of lies in the minds of men.

Santa is a lie, therefore Santa is Satan's son - and not his only son, but one of a multitude of offspring - antichrists who have been sired, incubated in, and born from the minds of men to compete with, and supplant the truth and reality of Jesus Christ.

Santa is Satan's brain child - as are all of the pagan myths and traditions, including Christmas, which so encrust the true Spirit of Christ - as indeed are all of the false gods, counterfeit religions and phoney Christian doctrines, traditions and ceremonies which have so occluded the true light of Christ from dawning in the hearts and minds of nations and generations of men, women and children for the last two millennia.

Around mid-September (**not December 25!**) about two thousand years ago in the town of Bethlehem, Jesus Christ was born in a stable where animals were fed and kept. Some time after the birth, Joseph, Mary and the infant Jesus moved into a house where they were visited (**up to two years later**) by an **unstated** number of wise men. Learned men who had been led to the infant Christ by a star in the sky - that Star of Bethlehem being the only one which God has ever encouraged mankind to follow.

And in light of what the birth of Christ represents to almost everyone who wrongly 'celebrates' it around the winter solstice, the perplexing thing is that those wise men did not go there to worship their own imperfect humanity - they didn't go to there to focus on, magnify and deify Mary and Joseph.

And neither did they travel to Bethlehem armed with their own 'carry outs' - with their own spiritual brews and concoctions intent on ignoring Christ and organising their own religious pomp and ceremony.

And having arrived, they didn't then proceed to exchange their gifts among themselves for their own self-gratification. No, they went there out of a real recognition of who the infant Jesus was, to pay homage to Him as God incarnate, and present their gifts to Him. Gifts which, in their giving, symbolised their recognition of Christ and His divine ministry - and the offering of their beliefs to Him.

And Satan, that murderer of reality, truth and life, knows the redeeming value of that simple gift of faith in Christ. And he knows it well. Which is why, even now in the bleak mid-winter of mankind's presence here on earth, he, together with his army of hellish, (s)elfish emissaries, are still working tirelessly away in some infernal grotto to inspire the production of all sorts of gaily coloured spiritual toys - alluring distractions - man-made facsimiles and virtual realities - religious amphetamines and barbiturates - spiritual hallucinogens and carcinogens - synthetic gods, counterfeit religions, spurious Christian doctrines, pagan myths, occult beliefs and woke philosophies - all to compete with, and if possible substitute themselves in the minds of mortals for the simple belief in the eternally redeeming truth of Christ's birth, His life, His sacrifice at Calvary and His resurrection.

And, in considering all of the manifesting, murderous aspects of Satan's hellish inspiration which now permeate and enslave our country - and which suppress the true Spirit of Christ at any time of the year, it has to be admitted that as far as 'New Age/Woke' Scotland is concerned:

SATAN aka SANTA RULES - OK

A week or so after my experience with the abandoned tabloid and while browsing the newspapers displayed on a supermarket stand, I caught sight of the front page of a tabloid which included a photograph of a child's letter.

The child was the eight-year-old son of Philip Lawrence - a schoolmaster who had been murdered several days previously in the grounds of his own school - St George's Roman Catholic School, Westminster. The letter was addressed to Santa/Father Christmas, and in it the youngster was asking Santa to give him his father back as a Christmas present.

If that child eventually succeeds in penetrating the dense curtain of myth and spiritual deception which was so occluding his spiritual perception at that time - if that boy eventually communicates directly with Christ, and not Santa or any of his spiritual siblings, then he will come to recognise the cruel and tragic irony which was conveyed in his letter - that irony being that it was Santa's two-faced, malignant and murderous influence working within our occult disposed, religiously godless, woke and spiritually blinded society which took his father's life in the first place.

CHAPTER TEN
Various Letters

To the Scottish People

There was a time, not so long ago, when the divine inspiration and spiritual integrity of the Holy Bible was generally accepted in this country as a matter of fact - but not so now.

There was a time, again not so long ago, when any religion, pseudo-Christian or otherwise, which disputed - and thus competed with the teaching and authority of the Holy Bible, would have been automatically and rightfully rejected in this country as spurious myth - but not so now.

And there was a time, yet again not so long ago, when those who practised and promoted occult beliefs would have been correctly judged by the people of this country to be the pedlars of hellish wares - but not so now.

Not so now is there any clear distinction among the people of this country between what is spiritually right and what is spiritually wrong.

And because there's no clear spiritual distinction - there's no clear psychological distinction, and because there's no clear psychological distinction - there's no clear moral distinction - and from this confusing mist the haunting spectre of lawlessness and social disintegration has long since started to materialise.

Not so now is the family unit of husband, wife and children held to be sacrosanct - or even normal or desirable!

Not so now is Scotland a just and peaceable country - or even one which is safe to live in!

Not so now are doctors and nurses safe in their hospitals - or even in their own surgeries!

Not so now are the young and old safe in the streets - or even in their own homes!

Not so now are children safe in their school playgrounds - or even in the classrooms!

Not so now is this nation distinctly, or even nominally Christian!

Not so now is white - white, or black - black, for in the minds of the people of this country, white has been relegated to, and black has been promoted to 'grey'. Grey is the colour of this country's corporate spirit - a 'politically correct' grey which darkens in tone as each day passes.

Grey Scotland, its government, its monarchy, most of its Churches, and the majority of its people have been lulled into a drunken stupor by accepting and consuming a spiked drink - an evil potion with an innocent look - a spiritually fatal concoction - a gaudy cocktail of just about every conceivable deceit which has ever been distilled in, and poured out from the vats of hell.

And while this once great country sleeps its drug induced sleep, it is in the process of drowning in its own vomit - the grey stinking puree of its own diet of spiritual compromise.

This country is ruled and influenced by grey people of compromise who, in relation to their own grey sphere of political and religious expediency, can be fairly judged as clever exponents, but who, in their relationship to the clear, sharp glare of the pure light of truth - in their relationship to Jesus Christ, can be rightly judged as uninformed dunces.

And they can, from the greyness of their *Sin* enslaved minds, produce their own 'alternative' gospels - their own 'political' solutions, their 'citizens' charters', their 'back to basics' policies, their 'new moral imperatives', and their 'progressive woke agendas'. And they can encourage and extol pluralism. And they can look to marry their own spiritually deceived and compromised state with every other spiritually deceived and compromised state. But none of it, **absolutely none of it,** will make any real difference to the relentless rise of evil in this country, because more compromise of God's Truth - more evil never was, and never will be an antidote for evil. The only effective antidote for evil is that which God Himself has prescribed - which is a pure, exclusive and **unadulterated** belief in His Son - Jesus Christ.

It is time the people of this country 'woke' up to the reality that this nation is terminally ill, and try as its leaders might - these political and religious sophists - these pretentious exponents of half-truths - these spin doctors don't have any real cures to offer anyone, **because there is no remedy apart from Jesus Christ.**

This country, this once strong man reposes terminally ill in his death bed. And as he lies there dying, he has a feed tube inserted into his mouth, and a drip tube intravenously connected to his right arm. At the moment the intravenous tube has been closed by a clamping device, and this sick old man is sucking desperately on the tube in his mouth - the tube being connected to a bottle whose narcotic contents are dark grey, and which carries a label marked 'more spiritual compromise'.

The other tube, the one which is attached to his right arm (but for the moment is clamped shut) is connected to a bottle which is suspended above his head, whose contents are blood red and which carries a label which states: 'Freely and selflessly given at Calvary for the regeneration of mortal life and the resurrection to eternal life'.

And the tragedy of this very real scenario is that the only reason that the life-giving transfusion isn't flowing into the sick old man's arm is that it is the vice like grip of his own hand which has clamped the tube. It is the patient's own continuing, deliberate and stubborn rejection of Christ which is killing him. Christ's feelings towards those who reject him are clearly expressed in **Matthew 23/37-38:**

O Jerusalem, Jerusalem, the one who kills the prophets and stones those who are sent to her! How often I wanted to gather your children together, as a hen gathers her chicks under her wings, but you were not willing! See! Your house is left to you desolate; ...

Jesus has provided the transfusion; He's even provided the intravenous tube - the spiritual umbilical - His Holy Spirit. All that any person, or any nation of people need do is spit out the tube in their ever-hungry mouth and, in releasing their **self**-determining grip on the artery of eternal life, receive Christ's blood - selflessly shed for their restoration.

If the people of this country seek real freedom, real safety, real security, real peace and prosperity in their lives, and the real assurance of eternal life with God in Heaven, then they, one and all, have no real choice to make, for the only God who can deliver reality in any sphere of existence is, not unnaturally, the only real God - Jesus Christ, which facts are consistently and clearly stated in the sixty-six books which constitute the Holy Bible.

Who will you choose to set free in your families, schools, communities and nation?

Jesus or Barabbas?

Your choice.

Yours <u>faith</u>fully

Jock Tamson

To the Scottish Government:

Dear Elected members,

I must admit that I don't really know where I'm going with this letter. But I do feel moved to write and, having just typed that confession, I now sit poised, hands hovering over the keyboard, fingers lightly tapping the keys, while I eagerly wait some cue - some opening - any opening which will allow me to continue to explore and express the deepening sadness which is burdening my soul.

You see members, it's like this, I've lost a friend - a good friend - a friend of real substance, one whom I had known throughout my life - and I need now, in some effective way, to give full vent to the anger which is lacing my grief - for by all accounts, my friend didn't need to die.

He had been there at my birth; he had helped me through the ill health of my pre-school years; he had taken a real and meaningful interest in my education; he had offered me firm and fixed guidelines on spiritual and moral matters, and he had given me a sense of identity, of belonging, of security and of well-being.

I struggle to remember when I last saw him - which might explain why I never really missed him. I must always have assumed he was there - there to be beckoned, there to be counted on, there to be enjoyed, but now, I realise, he's gone, and I grieve - oh, how I grieve!

And I don't know when he died either - I had heard that he was ailing - everyone knew that he had been suffering ill health for some time - but, nevertheless, the confirming reports of his death hit me hard.

The account of my dear friend's passing met me, as I slowly - and so very sorely, reflected on all of the newspaper pages which I had recently read. Most, if not all of the pages, bore coverage of his demise.

Classroom anarchy, knifings, robberies, horrendous murders, rapes, child molestation, violence, lawlessness, drug dealing and addiction, injustice, corruption, tyranny, treason - criminals and terrorists set free with innocents confined and intimidated.

My familiar friend - my accomplice - my sponsor - my kilted companion - my bastion of freedom, of justice, of decency, of marriage, of morality, of fidelity, of law and order, of rectitude, of good manners - my country - my Scotland had died.

And, as I further contemplated his passing, I realised that with his death had died the spiritual and moral values which he espoused and promoted

Furthermore, I continued to ponder, because my late, lamented Scotland's values remain my values, I have become a person without spiritual or moral relevance. I, a natural Scot by many generations, have become spiritually disenfranchised in my own land. The coinage of my soul has been withdrawn from circulation - my beliefs, my standards, my ethics - every single penny of my principles has been rendered 'illegal tender'. I have become an anachronism - as obsolete as a 'tanner' piece.

I can no longer transact - or converse - or share - I can no longer express one of the strongest aspects of my national identity without being called an ignorant bigot - or worse.

Why? because I am a Christian - exclusively and unashamedly so.

Yes, members - I believe Christ is who He said He is - with all the exclusion that implies.

And, I ask the question - is there a place for my voice in your 'new' Scotland?

Before you answer - let me attempt to defend this offensive Faith to which the vast majority of you pay no regard - this Faith, which was once the spiritual backbone of my late, lamented Scotland.

As I continue, please understand that I cannot defend any other religious beliefs because, except for Judaism, I have little interest in any other religion. My late Scottish friend only recognised and taught me to worship one God.

If you want Judaism defended, and defended as well as it can be - ask a Jew, if you want Islam defended, and defended as well as it can be - ask a Moslem, and if you want Hinduism defended, and defended as well as it can be - ask a Hindu etc., etc.

Anyway members, here is my humble contribution to the defence of the Christian faith.

Late one summer's evening, having returned to the car after walking my dog along the coastal path which stretches from the outskirts of Gourock to Inverkip Marina, I lingered to admire the view southwards over the widening Clyde estuary. From my vantage point at Lunderston Bay I could see Toward Point on the Cowal peninsula and, lying beyond that promontory, nestled the islands of Bute and Arran.

The vivid scene of hills and sky, of cloud and light - and of setting sun and silhouettes was awesome - and it raised within me a spontaneous prayer - a prayer of pleading - a prayer borne from a deep sense of incompleteness. My emotions had been engaged - overwhelmed and satiated by the splendour of that sunset scene, but my mind was left wanting - wanting to know and understand the origins - the spiritual origins behind that stunning interplay of landscape and light. And from that summer's evening in the late eighties - until the present, I believe that prayer has never stopped being answered.

I have been shown, in so many ways, and through so many sciences, that God's divine attributes - His sacrificial, triune nature - and His infinite power permeate and uphold the entire cosmos in a life sustaining state of equilibrium.

I have been taught that for every single thing (product) which has been created in the universe there is a creating process, and for every creating process, there is a creative prescription. Truly it is this functioning 'family unit' of Prescription, Process and Product which, through its different manifestations in **all** forms of life and reality, has created - and continues to sustain the entire universe.

As any physicist should confirm each prescription defines its purpose - or promised outcome and prescribes the processes to be actioned to achieve that purpose - or promised outcome.

In any context the ***Prescription*** can be seen as the genetic statement of intent – the ***'Let there be'***, and the ***Process*** can be seen as the active development, or '***the Letting there be'*** of that genetic statement, and the ***Product*** can be seen as the actual fulfilment, or the '***and there was'*** of the genetic statement of intent.

And to relate these factors to the triune God from whom they most definitely derive:

God, the Father - the legal, genetic prescription of eternal life - as given symbolic definition by, and through the lives and religion of the Jewish people - all as recorded in the Old Testament chapters of the Holy Bible.

God, the Son - the obedient and creative processing of the genetic prescription for eternal life - as enacted and embodied by Jesus Christ - all as recorded in the gospel narratives of the Holy Bible's New Testament.

God, the Holy Spirit - the promised fulfilment of the eternal relationship between God the Father - and God the Son - all as recorded in the Acts and the Epistles of the Holy Bible's New Testament.

It doesn't matter at what point in Creation the scientist might choose to look - he or she will always find this discreet triune relationship of Prescription, Process and Product working to create and uphold all things by its divine power.

Where life prospers - in **all** of its myriad biological and socially organised forms, the influence of God's triune nature - as lived through, and embodied in Jesus Christ will be seen to be freely operating, and where life is decaying or dead - the effects of that same trinity pattern will be seen to be diminishing, or non-existent.

Truly, to thwart and deny the Trinity - in whatever spiritual, psychological, physical or social realm it is operating, is to court disorder and constitutional breakdown.

To reiterate, nothing, absolutely nothing can be born - or introduced into this world except as the product - or child of the parental factors (genetic prescriptions and processes) which worked in tandem to produce it.

Nothing can infringe this universal law of divine origin - which is why, even Jesus Christ - the Son of God (in compliance with, and as promised by His Father's Eternal Law) had to come into this world as - a child.

It might be, Members, that you are starting to 'see the light' as far as the 'trinity' pattern is concerned, but....

might it also be, Members, that you still don't believe that Christ's sacrificial nature underpins the whole of creation?

If this is the case, then I defy you to take any idea which you have - any concept, no matter how simple or complicated - I challenge you to take that 'brain child' and transfer it from the conceptual to the actual without going through the process of expending yourself - without opening yourself and sacrificing your life's energy to the task.

It can't be done - you can't even draw breath without the sacrifice of life and energy! You see, Members, it takes a source of life and energy to create and sustain life and energy. Tell that to the humanists and atheists in your midst!

Everything which exists in the universe has come at a cost - there are no 'free tickets' in the real world - no conjurers - no magic spells - no alchemy – no phoney theory of evolution - everything which has been introduced into this world is the outcome of real sacrifice - everything, without exception, is a child of Calvary.

Prove me wrong, Members - I challenge you.

The truth is this - you can't even begin to prove me wrong - without proving me right.

Whether you like it or not, Members, whether it offends you or not, Christians believe that Christ enacted a universal truth at Calvary - He committed the absolute sacrifice - He paid the absolute price, so that He, and all who would subsequently believe in Him could experience gain - in this world, and the next.

It might be that other religions have Gods who, like Christ, have sacrificed their lives in a very real way so that their followers can enjoy a better life and an eternal future - I can express no opinion on the promises, or advantages of other religions.

All that I know is what my late lamented Scotland taught me - and taught me unashamedly, and that is this - that Christ paid the ultimate price to secure my ultimate destination.

And I also know this - when Christ's own people rejected Him 2000 years ago, it was not without consequence - for in choosing to reject and crucify Christ (life and peace) - they automatically elected to set Barabbas (lawlessness, injustice, tyranny and insurrection) - free to walk, and stalk their streets.

Members, what knife yielding, lawless, woke and disordering spirit walks - and stalks the streets and classrooms of your new Scotland?

Christ or Barabbas?

You don't know?

I suggest you start to read the same papers as I do.

If Christ enacted a universal truth at Calvary, then the Scottish people (once a Godly people) in rejecting Christ have confirmed another universal truth, and that is this: No individual, community or nation can reject God's grace - by whomever, and in whatever form it is presented, with impunity.

Members, it is my disenfranchised, Christian opinion (for what it's worth) that your 'new' Scotland, having turned away from Christ (God's grace), has impaled itself on the sword of God's wrath - and, under those circumstances, there is nothing - absolutely nothing that you, your party - or any cleverly devised election manifesto can do to trigger the revival of this nation.

Yes, Members, old Scotland is dead, and I grieve - and new Scotland?

It is the decaying, stinking corpse of old Scotland - a vile corruption of this once peaceable, well ordered and civilised country.

Truly, Members - I grieve over the death of my friend - my beloved Scotland.

Yours <u>faith</u>fully,

Jock Tamson

PS

Yes, old Scotland is dead - and no amount of 'progressive/woke' surgery will impart life to its decomposing cadaver.

The only effective solution is the re-establishment of the Christian Faith in this nation - thereby re-introducing God's only true prescription for the resurrection of this nation.

To 'King' Charles

Dear Charles,

Considering your obvious strong, self-preserving friendship with the religion of Islam (which denies Christ's divinity) allow me to enlighten you - as one who holds himself to be a true defender of the Christian Faith.

You must be aware that the religion of Islam is increasingly attempting to impose its values on our traditional way of life here in Scotland. But do you know that when Islam gains majority presence and influence in any country, it demands - and expects an unquestioning respect from those who do not follow its ways - and threatens those who insult its founder (Mohammed) with flogging, be-heading - or some other form of barbaric execution?

Do you recall the Charlie Hebdo murders in January 2015? - to mention just one example.

I don't know about you, Charles, but this poses a serious, life threatening problem to me - because, as a Scottish citizen of traditional descent, I find myself unable to practise the Faith of my choice without offering automatic insult to the followers of Islam - that offence being that I do not believe that Allah is the name of the true God, and neither do I believe that Mohammed was a prophet of the true God.

My beliefs render it **absolutely impossible** for me to extend spiritual or intellectual credibility to Mohammed, the Quran, the Hadith or any other tenet associated with Islam.

As a Christian - if I believe Jesus Christ's words, then **I must** discount Mohammed's words - I have no choice in this matter, absolutely none:

Christ claimed Divinity and, I believe, proved it by His resurrection after His crucifixion at Calvary - while Mohammed denied Christ's divinity and stated quite categorically in the Quran (Surah 4:156-159) that Christ was not crucified, and that His 'crucifixion' was some sort of stage-managed deception.

Christ claimed Sonship with God - while Mohammed relegated Christ to a mere messenger/prophet of Allah and stated, again categorically, and again in the Quran (Surah19:035) that God never had a Son.

Truly, if I believe Christ - I can offer no respect or credibility to Mohammed, Allah and Islam - absolutely none.

Christianity and Islam have been referred to in the past as 'great faiths' - but they both cannot be 'great faiths' because, as just indicated, one contradicts the other. Either one is 'a great faith' - and the other is a 'great lie' - or they are both 'great lies'.

The Jews have always believed the latter - that Christianity and Islam are both 'great lies' and, if nothing more, I admire their loyalty and constancy.

The Moslems - undoubtedly, have always believed that Christianity and Judaism are 'great lies' and, if nothing else, I acknowledge their stubborn intransigence.

The 'traditional' Christian establishments however, fearful of offending anyone, stutter and stammer, look down at their shuffling feet - while declaring, disloyally and pathetically, that there is much truth in all of the 'great' faiths - thereafter seeking to hide in spin and rhetoric that politicians would be proud to call their own.

There we have them - three of the 'great faiths' of the world, two are sustaining a low, apparently diminishing profile in this country, while the other, with its head high above the parapet, is increasingly attempting to impose itself and its 'sharia' law on the Scottish people.

But should a high profile, strident posture ever be assumed to be synonymous with spiritual integrity and rectitude?

Is Islam and its traditions due the automatic and absolute respect which it expects and demands from the Scottish populace - and, Charles, are you right in fostering such expectation and demand?

If Islam can prove to the Scottish nation that Allah is God and that Mohammed was his prophet - then, perhaps, it can expect and demand automatic and unconditional respect.

On the other hand - if Islam cannot produce the proof to substantiate Mohammed's claims for himself and Allah - then it shouldn't expect or demand any automatic respect from any free thinking, free speaking, civilised society.

Should it, Charles?

And, to be fair to Islam, that same challenge should be levelled at all of the 'great faiths' which circulate in this world.

If a God - or Gods cannot prove Himself, Herself or Themselves - then why should any person - or any nation of people be swayed by his, her or their 'divine' influence in the life of their community or nation?

In other words - as far as evidence for any particular God's existence is concerned - if the adherents of that God cannot 'put up' - then perhaps they should 'shut up' - and retire quietly to reflect on how fortunate they are to live in a society which protects their right to worship as they please.

Whether the Scottish people - 'your' people like it or not - they have a stark choice to make in respect to their attitude to these 'great faiths'.

This country must unify in its constitutional acceptance of, and loyalty to one of these 'great' faiths and (**if** the chosen faith allows) extend its benign tolerance to the residual minority - or unify in its constitutional rejection of all of these faiths and its tolerance of none.

To do otherwise will introduce this nation's psyche to a downward spiral of spiritual and cultural schizophrenia - where the voices of intolerance, hatred, madness, murder and mayhem will hold serious sway.

The last civilised nation to plummet to the schizoid state was (former) Yugoslavia - and the hellish, murderous consequences of that country's fall into fractured insanity are recent, historical fact - to which most people's memory can still freshly attest.

Truly this nation must act adroitly to preserve, defend and reinforce its traditional Christian culture - or face the dire consequences.

So, Charles, I know this would seem a needless question to ask the 'head' of the Church of England and 'Defender of the Faith' but I'll ask it anyway: To which religion - if any, should you and 'your' country <u>exclusively</u> ally itself?

Two of the main religions in this country are Christianity and Islam.

According to the Quran (Surah 5:073) Mohammed stated that it is blasphemy to say that Allah (God) is one of three in a Trinity.

According to the Holy Bible, God exists as the eternal Trinity of Father, Son and Holy Spirit (Matthew 28/19).

Again, according to the Holy Bible, men have no excuse for denying God's existence or wrongly identifying Him - because God has revealed His divine power and nature through the creation of the world as affirmed by **Romans 1:20**:

For since the creation of the world His invisible attributes are clearly seen, being understood by the things that are made, even His eternal power and Godhead, *(divine nature)* ***so that they are without excuse.*** *(brackets mine)*

So, whose nature is revealed, not in the mythical, muddy puddles of Creation's beginnings - but in the pure science of Creation's beginnings?

I don't know how many Laws of Physics have come into individual and concerted operation to create and sustain the Cosmos, perhaps Professor Stephen Hawking could have enumerated them, but however many there are - each and every one of these creative Laws comprise three inter-dependent partners.

For every creative Law (Prescription) - there is a compliant and active Process, and for every such Process - there is a Product. Truly it is the outworking of this tripartite relationship - this functioning 'family unit' of Prescription, Process and Product which, through its different manifestations in **all** forms of life and reality, has created - and continues to sustain the entire universe.

As any physicist should confirm each Prescription defines its purpose - or promised outcome and prescribes the processes to be followed to achieve that purpose - or promised outcome.

In any context the Law can be seen as the prescriptive initiative, or genetic base (with its intrinsic promise); the Process can be seen as the active and obedient development of that genetic base, and the Product can be seen as the (promised) result of the co-operation between the compliant Process and its initiating Law.

And to relate these factors to the triune God from whom they most definitely derive:

God, the Father - God's inherent and absolute knowledge of who He is (and who He isn't) - the immoveable foundation of, and essential description of His eternal being - the definitive, genetic prescription of His eternal life - as presented through, and illustrated by the Law and prophets (promises) of the Old Testament.

God, the Son - God's obedient and perfect processing - or true expression of the genetic prescription of eternal life - as presented through the birth, the life, the self sacrifice and the resurrection of Jesus Christ - all as faithfully recorded in the Gospels of the New Testament

God, the Holy Spirit - God's complete power - the true, perfect, full and active expression of His eternal Truth, Life and Love - the promised fulfilment of the relationship between God the Father and God the Son - as epitomised by Christ's resurrection, and exemplified in the Epistles of the New Testament.

It doesn't matter at what point in Creation the scientist might choose to look – he or she will always find that discreet triune relationship of Prescription, Process and Product working to create and uphold all things by its divine power:

Nothing, absolutely nothing of real life and integrity can be born - or introduced into this world except as the product - or child of the parental factors (genetic prescriptions and processes) which worked in tandem to produce it. Nothing can infringe this universal law of divine origin - which is why Jesus Christ - the Son of God, in compliance with His Father's Eternal Laws and promises had to come into this world as a child.

Where life prospers - in all of its myriad biological and socially organised forms, the influence of God's triune nature - as lived through, and embodied in Jesus Christ will be seen to be freely operating, and where life is decaying or dead - the effects of that same trinity pattern will be seen to be diminishing, or non-existent. Truly, to thwart and deny the trinity - in whatever spiritual, psychological, physical, social or national realm it is operating, is to court the cancer of disorder and constitutional breakdown.

Our society is breaking down - every other news bulletin confirms this nation's decline into lawlessness, deception and disorder. Nobody can refuse to acknowledge the spiritual, moral and social decay which is taking place in our land - it is so, so plain to see.

So Charles, and please don't take this too personally, I believe that the **only** cure for this nation's terminal sickness is that its ailing and corrupt government dismisses all false religions - and thereafter re-embraces an exclusive belief in the only **true source of spiritual power and authority** in Heaven and Earth, who is, who was, and who always will be:

Our Father in heaven,
Hallowed be Your name.

Your kingdom come.
Your will be done
On earth, as it is in heaven.
Give us this day our daily bread,
And forgive us our debts,
As we forgive our debtors.
And do not lead us into temptation,
But deliver us from the evil one.
For Yours is the kingdom, and the power and the glory.
for ever. Amen.

If our Father God - our true King will only convey His creative power and authority from Heaven to earth through recognition of, and belief in His Son (the divinely sanctioned process) - what chance does a nation have whose Monarchy, Government, Churches and Institutions continually disregard, devalue, supplant, malign, denigrate and even criminalise that graciously given process?

What chance, Charles?

A snowball's chance in Hell.

Yours sincerely,

Jock Tamson

And finally, a word from Jesus as recorded in John 6/38-40.

…For I have come down from heaven, not to do My own will, but the will of Him who sent Me. This is the will of the Father who sent Me, that of all He has given Me I should lose nothing, but should raise it up at the last day. And this is the will of Him who sent me, that everyone who sees the Son and believes in Him may have everlasting life; and I will raise him up in the last day.

www.ingramcontent.com/pod-product-compliance
Lightning Source LLC
Chambersburg PA
CBHW071221070526
44584CB00019B/3104